ULTIMATE EYE TWISTERS

Archimedes Laboratory™

ULTIMATE EYE TWISTERS

A Mesmerizing Mass of Optical Illusions

CARLTON KIDS

Archimedes Laboratory™

This is a Carlton book

Editor: Joff Brown
Art Editor: Deborah Vickers
Designer: Samantha Richiardi
Creative Director: Clare Baggaley
Production: Nicola Davey

Pages 6-96 from original book entitled Eye Twisters,
artworks and Text © Carlton Publishing 2013

Pages 97-183 from original book entitled Eye Bogglers,
artworks and text © Gianni A. Sarcone,
giannisarcone.com 2011, 2018

Eye Bogglers first published in 2011 and Eye Twisters
first published in 2013 by Carlton Books Limited,
an imprint of the Carlton Publishing Group,
20 Mortimer Street, London W1T 3JW

10 9 8 7 6 5 4 3 2 1

A catalogue record for this book is
available from the British Library.

ISBN: 978-1-78312-448-0
Printed in Dubai, UAE

GET READY...

Your eyes – those incredible jelly balls beneath your forehead – capture everything around you. They are sense organs allowing you to see, and they give more information about your surroundings than any of the other four senses: hearing, taste, touch and smell.

But what you see also depends on your brain. It receives electrical signals from the eyes and uses these to make sense of what is seen. But the brain also adds two extra ingredients of its own: memory and meaning.

It is because of these extra two things that the brain is sometimes tricked by the eyes. When you see something that is not really there, or something different from what is really there, you are experiencing an optical illusion.

This book is intended to surprise and entertain, and also to encourage you, dear reader, to always look beyond what you see… Have fun!

Archimedes Laboratory™
Researchers and artists

Impossible Cube

Sometimes you can draw an object that would be impossible to make in three dimensions. Can you draw a cube like this one?

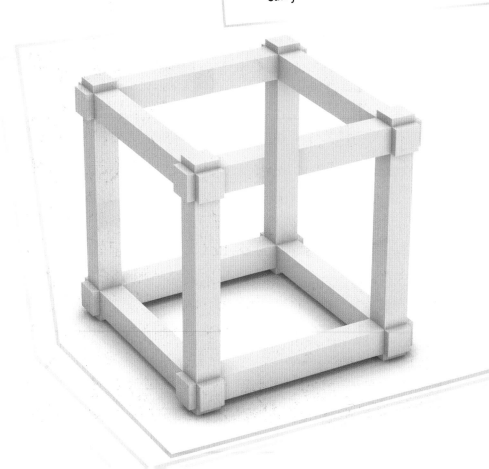

Scintillating Grid

Look for the dots – but not too hard,
or they'll vanish!

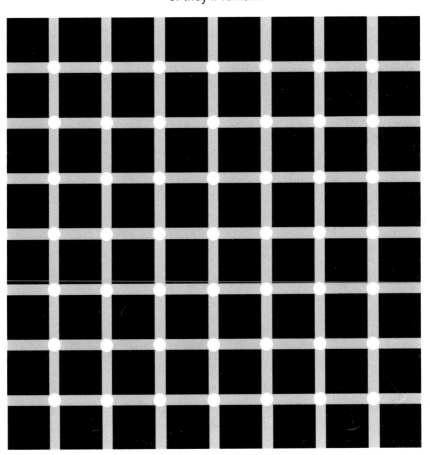

Interlocking Impossibilities

Have the cubes from page 6 been breeding?

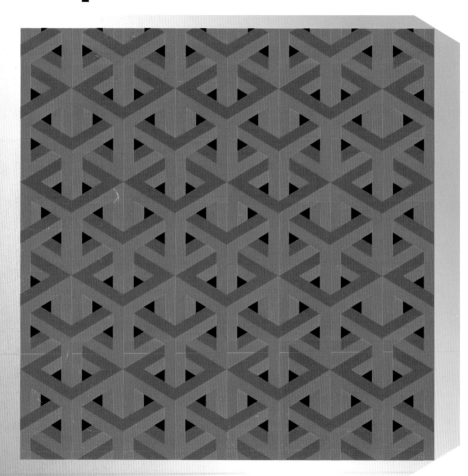

Pulsating Purple

Is this a crumpled paper napkin, or pulsating waves of colour?

Standing Spin?

Are these men standing still or dancing in endless circles?

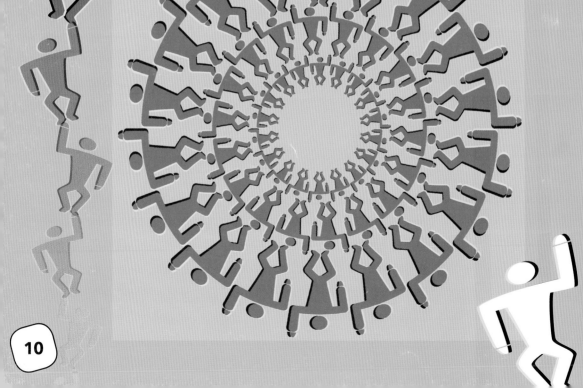

Convex or Concave?

Are you looking at the top of a pyramid, or peering down a tunnel?

Corner Quandary

Are these cubes bulging out at you, or bending in? Can they do both?

Bogus Bulge

The gradually changing shapes mimic a flat piece of paper that bulges. So a bulge is what you see!

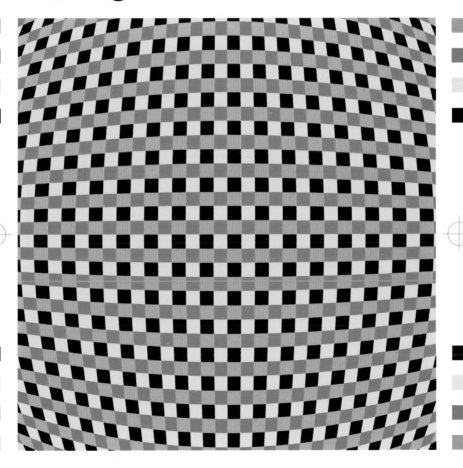

Try This One at Home!

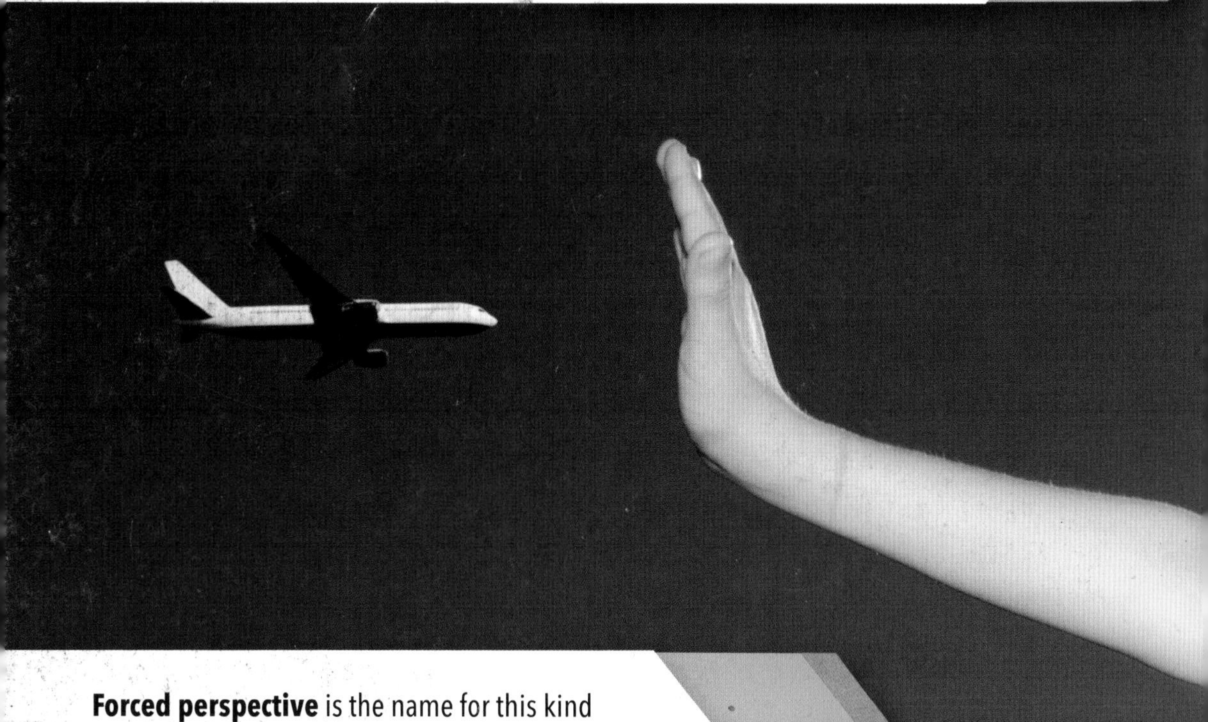

Forced perspective is the name for this kind of image, where a huge object looks tiny because it's shown next to something much smaller but also closer to the camera.

Can you set up your own photo like this one in your back garden or school playground?

14

15

Eternal Turning

The wheels spin slowly and endlessly - until you look
directly at one of them. Then that one stops!

Girls or Glass?

In this classic illusion, do you see a fancy glass goblet, or
two faces about to kiss?

Twitching Tree

Are these leaves hanging motionless on a hot day, or waving in a cool breeze?

Which Windows?

This is a very strange block of flats. Are those windows,
skylights or holes in the floor?

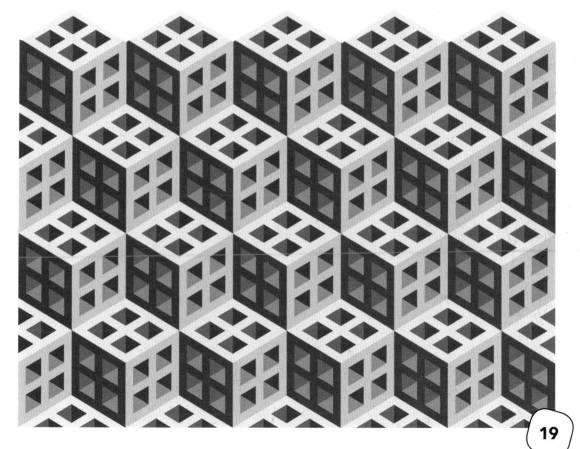

Fruit Fool?

This is an ordinary picture of a basket of fruit... until you turn it upside down.

Inwards or Outwards?

Multiple waterfalls of chocolate sliding into infinity, or a mud pie explosion – which is it?

Spot the Petal

Can you see petal shapes in this amazing image? Or are there just black and white squares?

Count the Cubes

Can you pick out seven big cubes in this picture? Some of them are only partly visible.

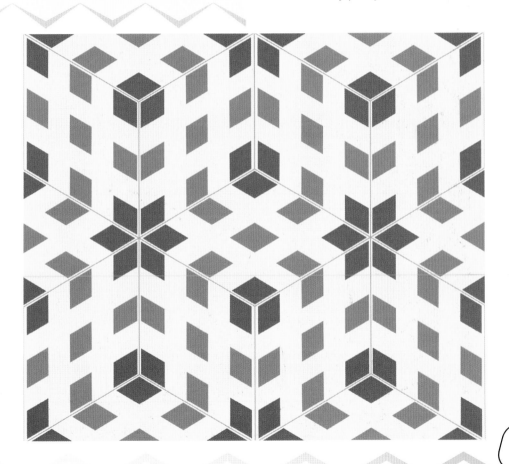

Seeing Stars

Stare at this circling illusion and the outer stars turn clockwise while the inner ones go the other way!

Dicing with Dimensions

This cube of dice is a more complex version of the illusion on page 6. Can you draw this one too?

Squaring the Circle

Are these squares and rectangles flat or domed?

Flower Bursts

Sit back and watch the flowers grow
before your very eyes!

Stationary Shuffle

It's the dancers from page 10 again. Are they lying down for a rest, or wriggling across the sand?

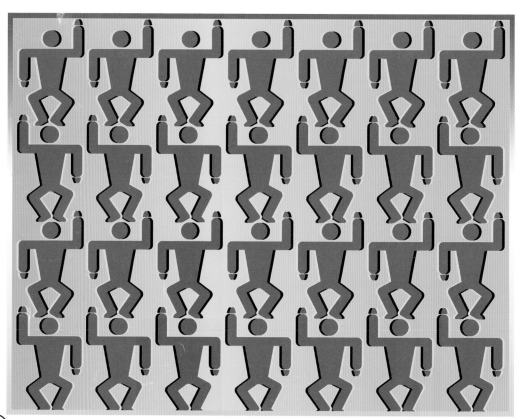

Try
This
One
at
Home!

You don't need to visit the Leaning Tower of Pisa to set up a picture like this – try it with a large tree.

Street Seen?

Can you spot which parts of this street scene are real, and which are painted on a blank wall?

Sun Shock

The waves coming out of the sun here seem to almost jerk in and out as your eye expects to see one thing but actually sees another, and quickly adjusts.

Line Up the Lines

Are the lines between the squares straight or bendy?
Your ruler may disagree with your eyes!

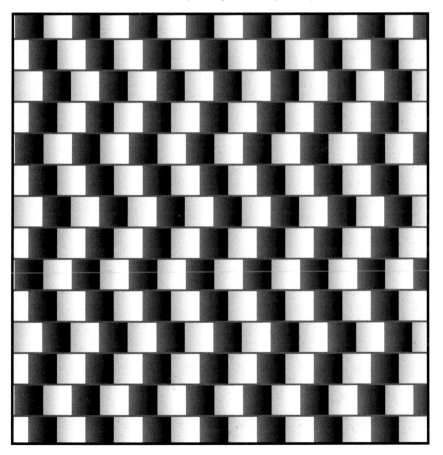

Sky Teaser

Can you guess what this is?
The answer is at the back of the book.

Two Ways at Once

This circling image seems to move in jerks.
Is the motion clockwise or anticlockwise?

Checkerboard Warp

Can you follow an alternating series of black and white squares from one side of the page to the other without blinking?

Floored!

This clever painting makes it appear that a hole in the room's floor goes through to a similar room below.

Try This One at Home!

Here's another one you can reproduce yourself. Get your friend to stand far away from you, hold up your hand and take a picture of the result.

Rhombuses, Really

It's easy to see this image as three-dimensional cubes, but can you see it as two-dimensional rhombuses? (A rhombus is a four-sided shape where all sides have equal length.)

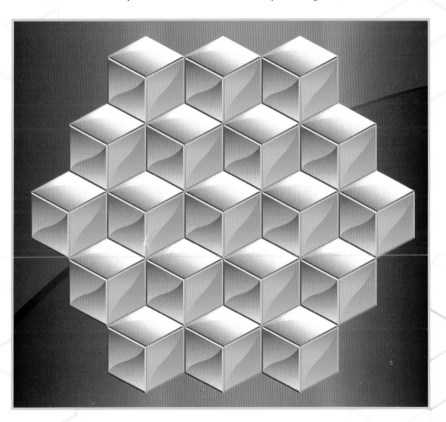

Rainbow Rays

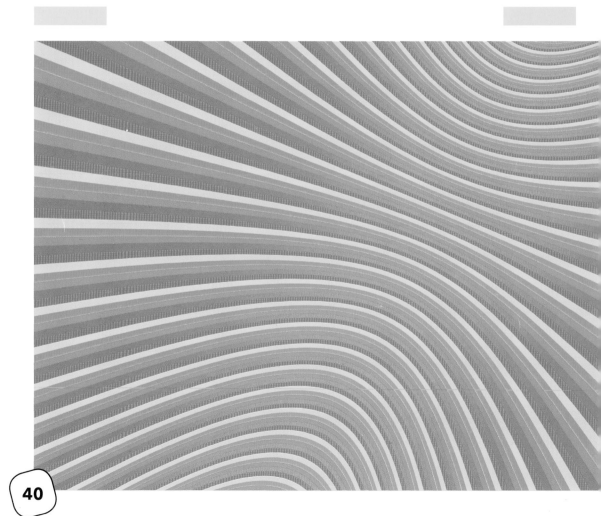

Are these lines bending inwards or outwards? When you stare at
the point where they bend, can you see a shimmering effect?

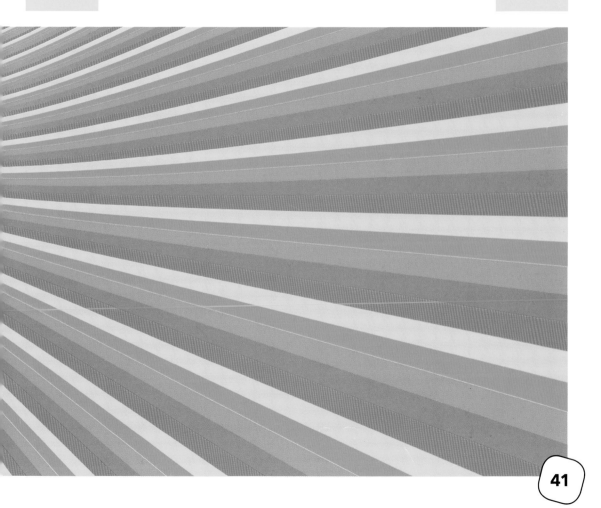

Cracked?

Your brain thinks it knows what a building looks like,
and persistently 'corrects' your eye when it tells you
that this construction is impossible!

Wheels within Wheels

How many different circles of movement can you see at once? Usually just the outer two circles seem to move, but can you spot the inner ones moving?

Window or What?

You've probably guessed this isn't a real window. But what is it? The answer is at the back of the book.

Merged 'Z's

Do you see a light grey forwards 'Z'
or a black backwards one?

Twisting Test

How long can you stare at the spinning circle without having to blink? Time yourself!

Balancing Act

Who do you think will fall off first?

Mangled Mechanism

Not only would these wheels never turn in real life, but you could never build them in the first place.

Afterimages

Stare at the white dot for 30 seconds, then close your eyes. What do you see?

These afterimage portraits by Dimitri Parant work by overstimulating some cells in the eye and understimulating others.

Laser Lights

This moving illusion consists of the pattern made
by a reflected laser beam.

Wink at Me

If you look at this illusion with one eye instead of both, it may move less or not at all. This is because with only one eye in play your brain is receiving less contradictory information.

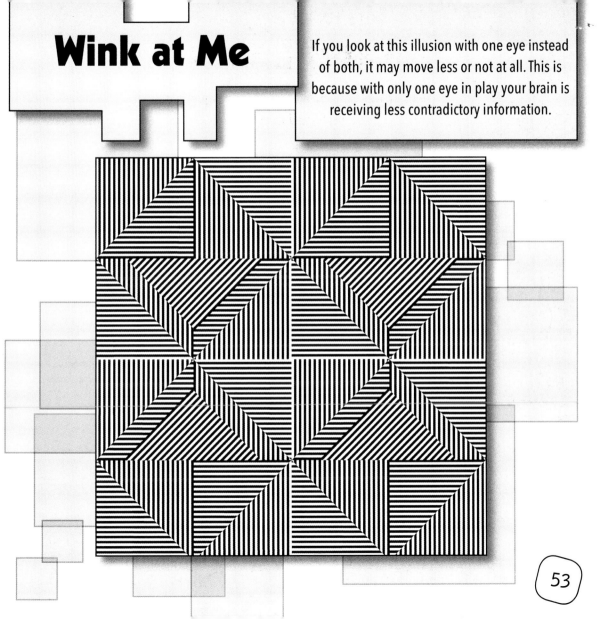

Side Street

This building in Spain invites you to stroll... through a brick wall!

Eternity Ring

This simple illusion has no beginning and no end, but it looks as if you could wear it on your finger.

Spinning Tunnel

The 'V's seem to circle endlessly. But do the ones on the red streak seem to move less than the others?

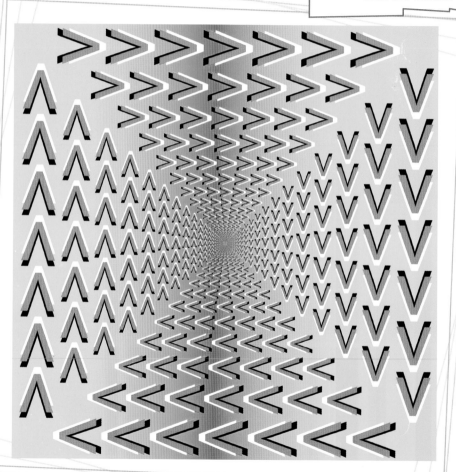

Penguin Playground

This construction creates an 'impossible reality'.

Plumbing The Heights

This is not actually an optical illusion, but a real sculpture in Ypres, Belgium.

Bursting Bulge

This illusion is a more protruding version of the Bogus Bulge on page 13.

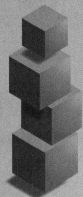

Cube Accumulation

In this kind of image, each cube looks entirely realistic on its own – but they add up to something much less likely.

Who are We?

The princess and her grumpy stepmother... or the other way around?

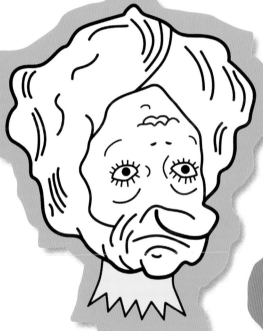

Try This One at Home!

You might not have a bird bath the size of the one outside this Bavarian castle, but why not hold a dish in front of your house so that the house 'sits' on it?

ELECTRIC AVENUE

If you stand in the right place, this piece of street art in Poland looks three-dimensional.

Stretching Credibility

This sculpture at Cairo airport is possible because the 'rocks' are actually made of a paper-mache-like material.

Old or Young?

This optical illusion was printed on a German postcard in 1888.
Do you see an old lady looking sideways.. or a young lady looking away?

Calm Centre?

By focusing on the absolute centre, can you make this pulsing image stay still?

Straighten Me Out

If you removed two cubes from this figure, it would cease to be an illusion. Can you work out which? The answer's at the back of the book!

Wiggin Out!

Cyclist Bradley Wiggins comes face to face with jungle street art created by Kurt Wenner.

Try This One at Home!

Who do you want to step on?
Make sure they get a turn at stepping on you too!

Hanging Around

Artist Leandro Erlich painted a housefront on the ground and hung a huge mirror above it so people could lie down and see themselves 'suspended' from the walls!

Port Cut

Did this homeowner chop through their wall
to provide quick access to the beach?

Sewer Surprise

Turtles erupt from a fake sewer in this street art by 3D Joe and Max.

Try This One at Home!

You could set up this shot in your local park. Or, if you live in a flat with a balcony, you could replace your arm with the balcony bottom!

Try This One at Home!

Squirming Circle

Can you count the 'V's in the centre circle, or do they squirm too much? The answer is at the back of the book.

Suspension of Disbelief

The 'natural' way the light is depicted here fools the eye into thinking this image should work like a real shelf.

Shifting Sands

Do you see a desert scene, a dog or a face? Or all three?

Pulsating Black Hole

The blue lozenges rush to be swallowed up, but never actually get there.

Try This One at Home!

Is anyone in your family annoyingly tall?
Set up this photo to cut them down to size!

80

Spider Sense

This amazing art is drawn on a flat surface but looks like a deep canyon between buildings when viewed from the right spot.

Marvellous Marble

This marble spins without
needing to be pushed!

Water Boggler

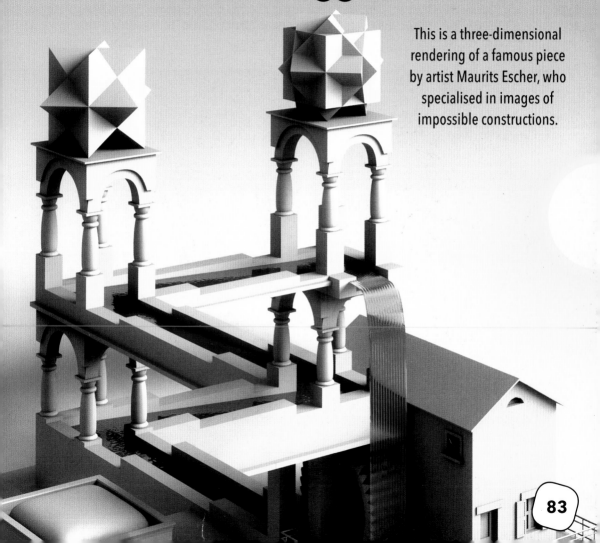

This is a three-dimensional rendering of a famous piece by artist Maurits Escher, who specialised in images of impossible constructions.

The Big City

A model city? No, this is a real suburb of Istanbul, captured with tilt-shift photography, which creates a blur around the edge of an image and sharpens the centre.

Endless Climb

Can you make these impossible stairs out of paper?
Then, can you take a photo at an angle that makes it look real?

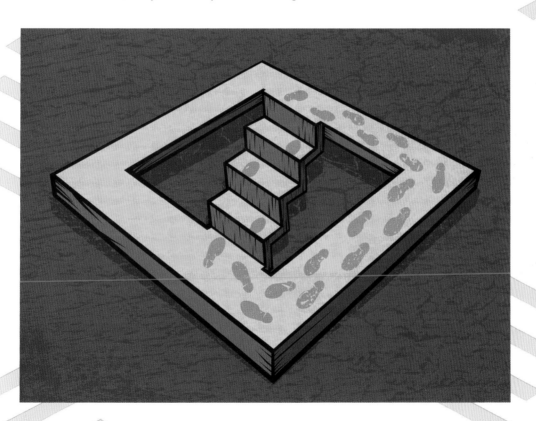

Magic Mosaic

This two-dimensional image seems to move like the beads in a kaleidoscope. (If you don't know what that is, ask your parents!)

The Parrowdox

Try copying this drawing. First do the lines, and then the shading. Can you see how the shading strengthens the three-dimensional effect?

Undulating Paper

This illusion uses the bulge effect seen on pages 13 and 59 to create an effect of multiple undulations, or waves.

Breaking Bounds

Because we are so used to seeing pictures within frames, a picture that spills over looks like a real object. Here the tiger, the frame and the shadow are all painted.

Ghost Images

These negatives of Clark Cable and Greta Garbo work similarly to the afterimages on pages 49 to 51. Stare at the four white dots for 30 seconds, then shut your eyes.

91

Arrow Wrap

Is the green arrow bent or straight?

Try This One at Home!

This woman is facing a large mirror. If you place two mirrors opposite each other, you can create a series of never-ending reflections.

Find The Rabbit

Can you find the head of a rabbit in this old illustration of a hawk? The answer is at the back of the book.

Downside Up?

Is this a man with a beard and strange hair... or a man with a beard and strange hair?!

Dotty Circles

Scan your eyes across these circles. Can you see little brown dots start to appear and disappear all over the pattern?

The Impossible Vault

Does this door open
outwards or inwards?
Your money wouldn't
be very safe in here!

© G. Sarcone, www.archimedes-lab.org

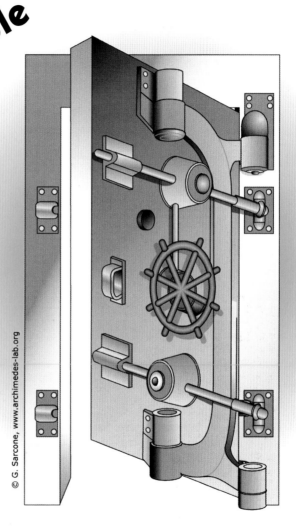

Arrow

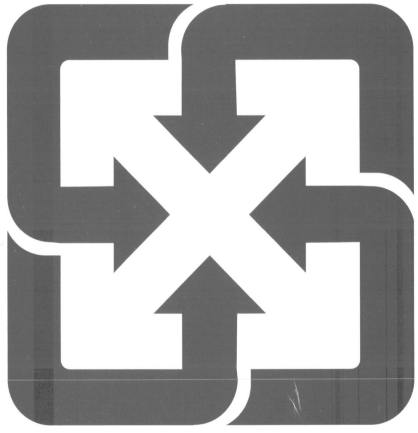

How many arrows can you see? Are you sure? Count them again…
(Answer at the back of the book)

Ant Army

Without counting them, are there more red ants or white ants?
(Answer at the back of the book)

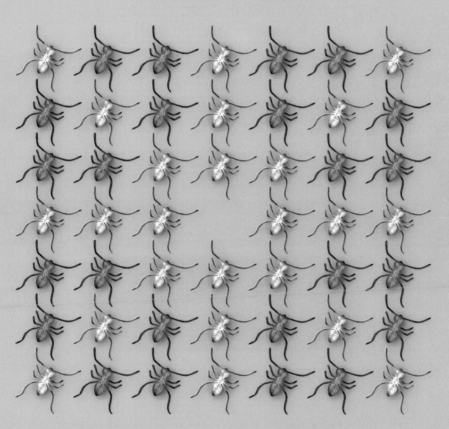

Light or Heavy

Which of these elephants is heavier?
(Answer at the back of the book)

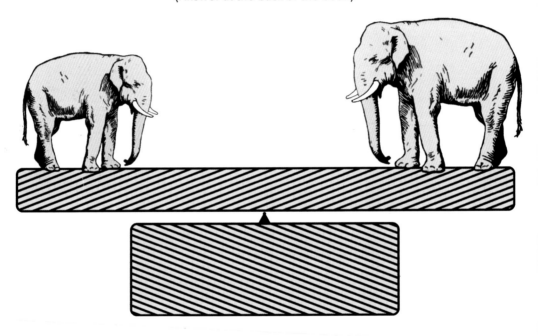

Crazy Wavy

The lines in this picture might look wavy…

But are they? (Answer at the back of the book)

Famous Face

Start by looking at this picture close up. Slowly move the book away from you until a face appears. Who is it? (Answer at the back of the book)

Spaghetti Twist

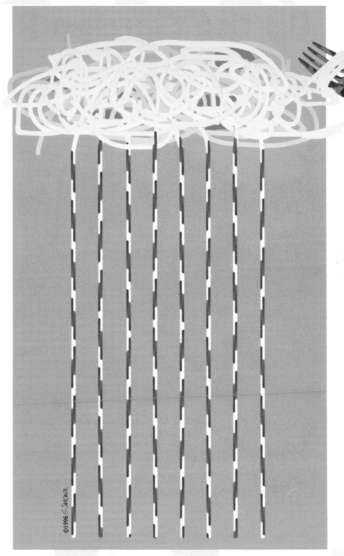

Does the hanging, striped spaghetti bulge inwards or outwards?
(Answer at the back of the book)

Up the Garden Path

Follow the paths… Which is the longest: A to B or A to C?
(Answer at the back of the book)

Van Cram

Can you fit all these boxes into the van?
Try tracing the boxes onto a piece of paper, cut them out and see
if you can make them fit. (Answer at the back of the book)

Hidden in the Petals

Can you find an animal hidden in this rose?
(Answer at the back of the book)

All Alone?

Is this old lady really alone? How many people can you see with her?

Face of Fruits

The artist who painted this clever portrait using fruit and vegetables
also painted people made of books, flowers and even fish!

Towering Temples

Which of the temples is taller, A or B?
(Answer at the back of the book)

Shhh, Someone's Listening!

The man reading the book appears to be on his own, but is he?
Can you see who's with him? (Answer at the back of the book)

Could you bathe at this beach?
Follow the shoreline and see…

Above

or Below?

Notice anything strange? The way this structure is drawn means you can look up at one man, while looking down at the other!

Dog

or Cat?

Hidden in this picture is a very ugly dog and a cute cat.
Can you find them both? (Answer at the back of the book)

Sea Legs

At first glance this might seem like a normal line of sailors, but look carefully...
Can you see something strange going on with their legs?

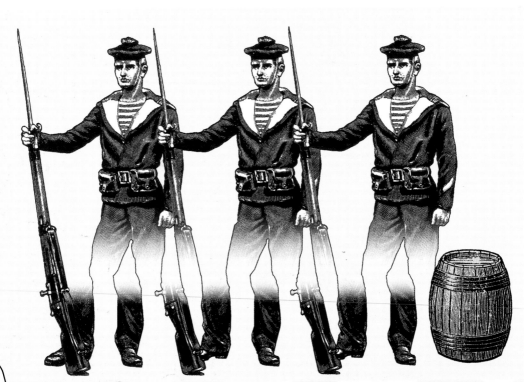

Spot the Spots

Glance across these buildings. Can you see grey dots appearing and vanishing where the window frames meet each other?

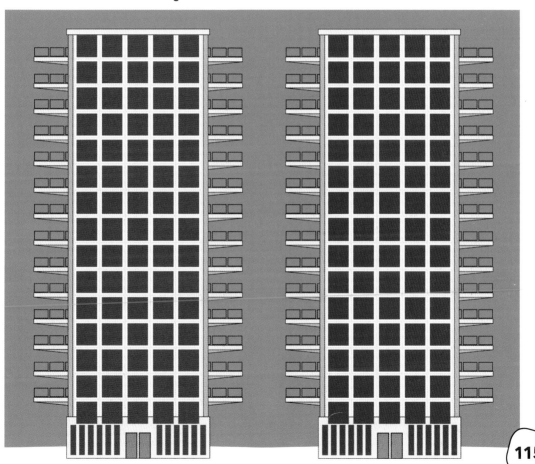

Golden Dome

Which two colours make up the golden dome on this building?
Look carefully, you may be surprised!
(Answer at the back of the book)

A   **B**

C   **D**

Stripe Selection

Can you tell which bar (A or B) matches the bar in the red and green box?
(Answer at the back of the book)

A

B

Bendy Legs

Look very carefully. Are the legs of these funny-looking men straight or bent?
(Answer at the back of the book)

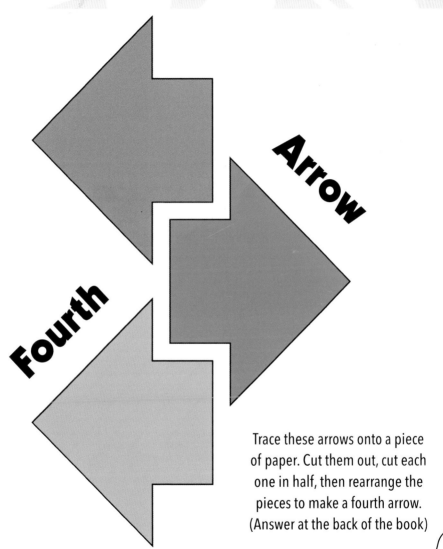

Fourth Arrow

Trace these arrows onto a piece of paper. Cut them out, cut each one in half, then rearrange the pieces to make a fourth arrow. (Answer at the back of the book)

Going Up!

Whatever direction these men are facing they always seem to be going up. How will they ever get down!

Tilting Squares

These squares look as if they are tilting to the left
when they are actually perfectly upright.

A Foxy Puzzle

There are more animals than you think in this picture. See if you can find a boar, a horse and a lamb hidden in the undergrowth. (Answer at the back of the book)

The Floating Vase

What do you see? A shadow under a floating vase
or just a stain on the tablecloth?

If you move your eyes round and round this clock the cogs will start to look as if they are moving.

Cat or Mouse ?

This cat is looking for a mouse. Can you find it?

Shrinking

Relax and look at the centre of this picture. You should start to see the purple discs move towards the centre of the circle.

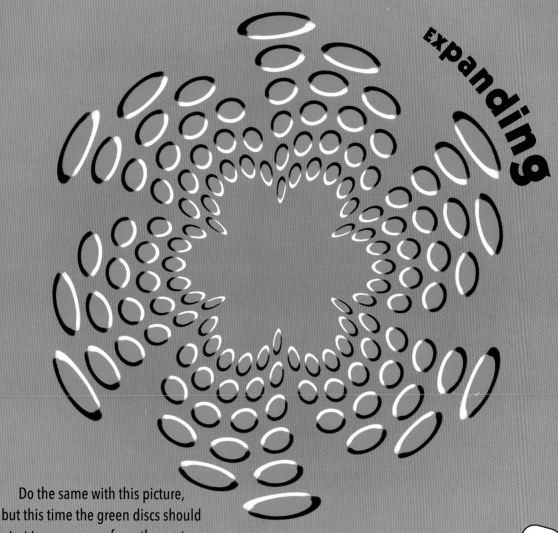

Do the same with this picture,
but this time the green discs should
start to move away from the centre.
Remember to stay relaxed!

Hidden Baby

Can you help the mother
panda find her baby?
(Answer at the back of the book)

Lonely Dancers

These dancers are having fun, but are they really alone?
(Answer at the back of the book)

Carpet Capers

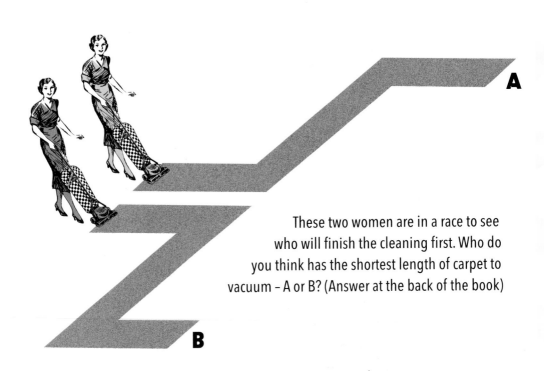

These two women are in a race to see who will finish the cleaning first. Who do you think has the shortest length of carpet to vacuum – A or B? (Answer at the back of the book)

Where You Bean?

Can you find a child's face hiding in these coffee beans? (Answer at the back of the book)

Circling Cards

Focus on the cross in the middle and move the book towards and away from you. Do you notice anything strange?

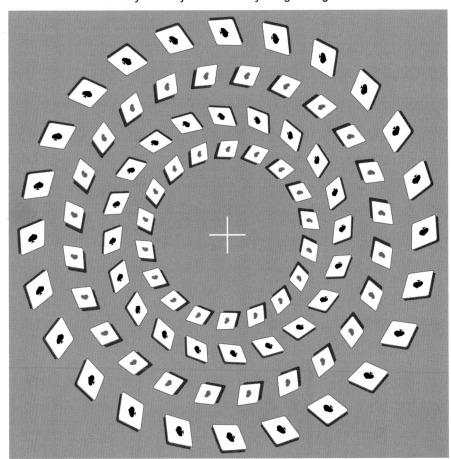

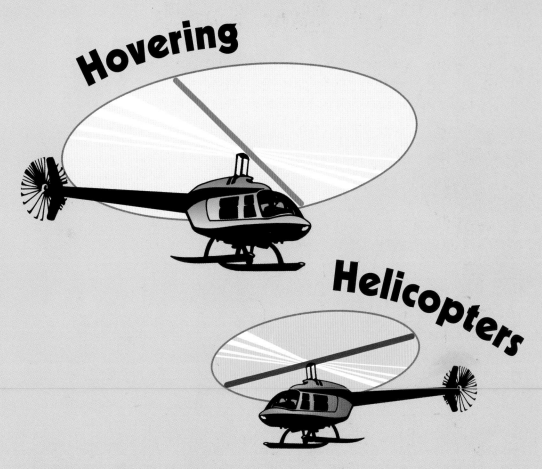

Hovering Helicopters

Look carefully at both of these helicopters.
Which line is longer: blue or red?
(Answer at the back of the book)

Tall
and
Small

Which of these men is the tallest? Mind you don't get caught out! (Answer at the back of the book)

Shooting Stars

Relax and concentrate on this picture. The stars should start to pulsate and the white background should turn slightly blue.

How Many Angels?

How many angels can you see in this picture?
(Answer at the back of the book)

Jiggling Jellyfish

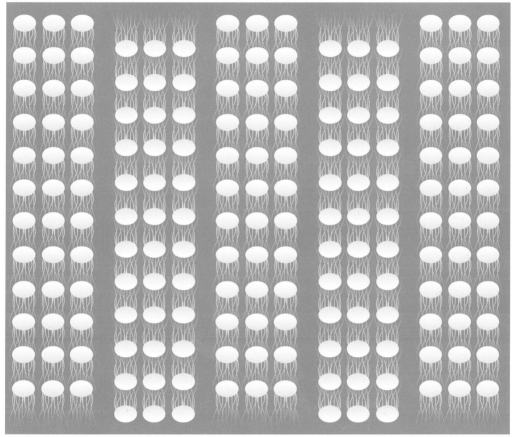

Imagine you are looking at a sea of jellyfish. Stare at the picture then move your eyes around the groups and the jellyfish will start to move.

Spooky Face

Stare at this picture until a rather spooky hidden face starts to appear.

Bear or Seal?

Is this a bear crawling out of a hole in the ice or a seal enjoying a rest?

Black or White

Is this a white wall being painted black or a black wall being painted white?

Chicks in the Nest

Can you find ten birds within this picture?
(Answer at the back of the book)

The Perfect Circle?

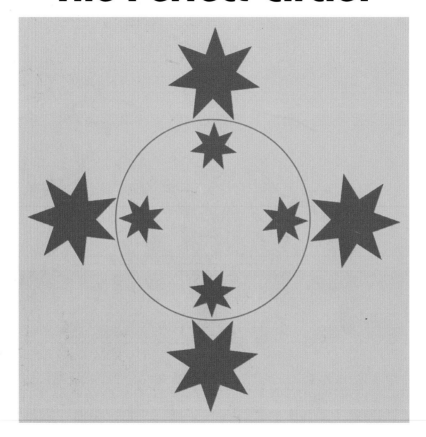

Is this circle perfectly round?
(Answer at the back of the book)

Faces

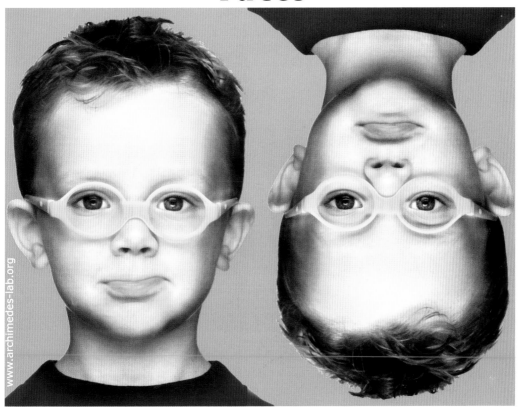

Faces

Without turning the book upside down, find two differences between these boys.
When you've given up you can turn the book around!

143

A Very Odd Place

There are five crazy things going on in this picture, can you find them all?
(Answer at the back of the book)

Crazy Car

Do you think you could drive this vehicle?

Towering Man

This man looks taller that the Eiffel Tower, but he is larger because he is closer to the camera. These sort of pictures are easy to set up, so why not try it with your own camera?

Impossible Stairs

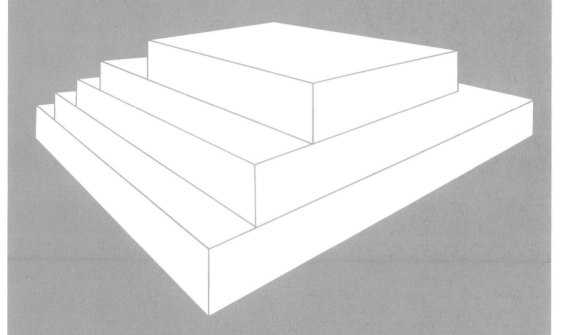

Only two stairs on the right and five stairs on the left! How does that happen?

Lady in the Landscape

A sailing boat through some trees on a dark night, or a woman's face?
(Clue: the boat is her nose and mouth.)

Seal Shapes

If you turn the seal upside down, can you see a bird?

Tiger Tiger

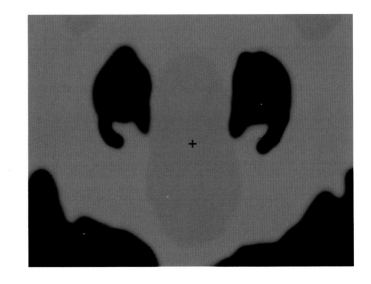

Stare at the cross
in the blue picture
for 15 seconds,
then quickly stare
at the cross in
the tiger picture.
What happens?
(Answer at the back
of the book.)

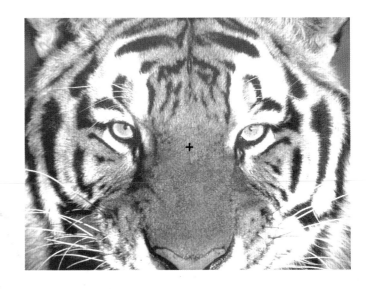

Hidden Faces

Can you see the faces outlined by the sides of these cups? They are frowning, sticking their tongues out and laughing at each other!

Keep on Climbing

Could you get to the top of these stairs?

Rotating Rings

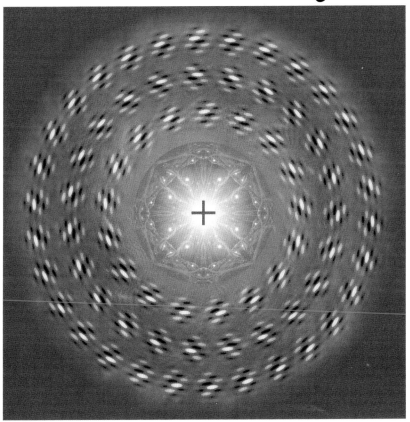

Focus on the cross in the middle of the circle then move the book away from you and towards you. Be careful, it could make you dizzy!

A World of Hair

JAMES MONTGOMERY FLAGG

Hidden in this map of the world is the face of a girl with lots of hair. Can you see her?

All Tied Up

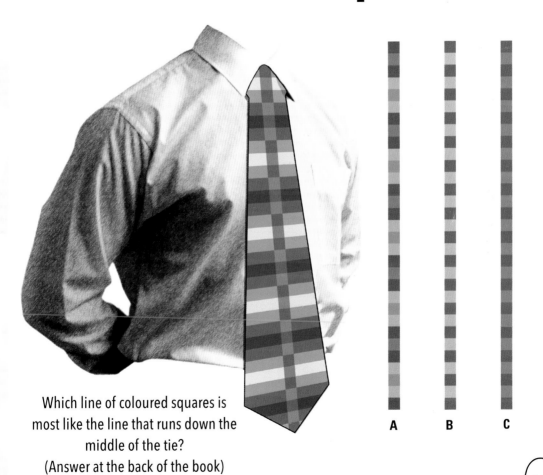

Which line of coloured squares is most like the line that runs down the middle of the tie?
(Answer at the back of the book)

The Impossible Building

How could the woman knock a flower pot off her windowsill? This building could never exist!

Box Clever

Give the boxers a ring! Draw a
square that connects all eight dots.
(Answer at the back of the book)

The Magic Glass

Can you take one of these glasses off the tray?
(Answer at the back of the book)

Crawling Creepers

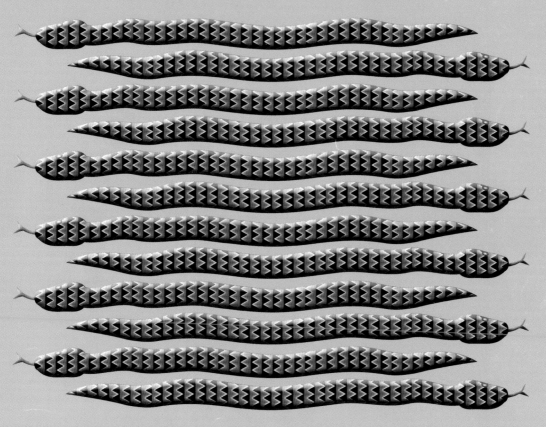

Stare at these slithery snakes for while before moving your gaze around the picture. The snakes will look as if they are wriggling on the page.

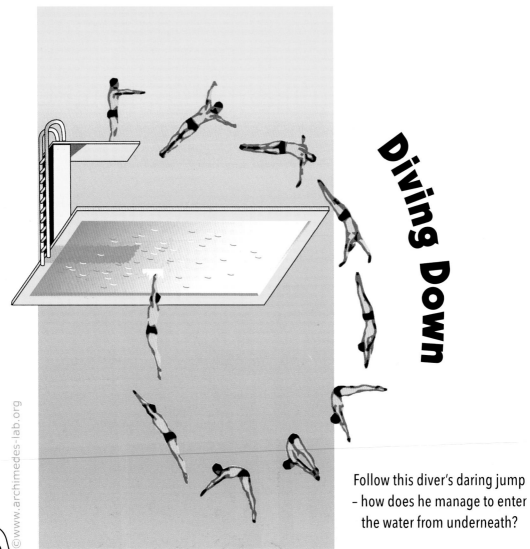

Diving Down

Follow this diver's daring jump
– how does he manage to enter
the water from underneath?

Phantom Tomato

Is this a tomato on a plate or just the stalk on an empty plate? Count the prongs on the fork, how many does it have? Are you sure?

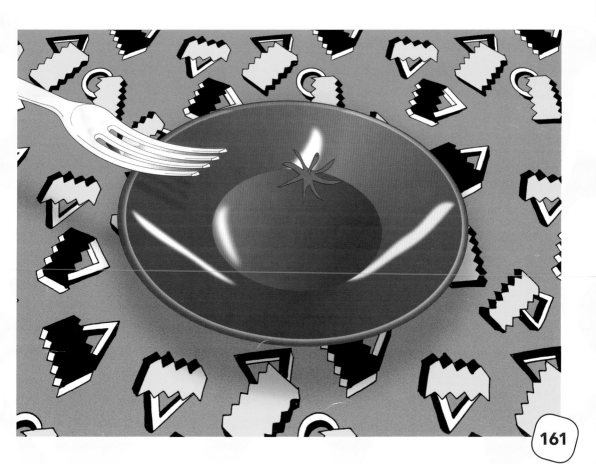

Under the Arches

These arches don't look quite right.
Can you see what is wrong with them?

What Is It?

Can you guess what this picture is? There is no right or wrong answer and your guess might even be funnier than our suggestion. (Answer at the back of the book)

Off-Colour Cow

The colour in this picture is not balanced. Can you see that there is more blue on one side and more yellow on the other? To balance the colour, stare at the fly in the second picture for 30 seconds, then look at the cow again.

© 1998, Gianni A. Sarcone, www.archimedes-lab.org

Guess the Picture

Have a guess at what this picture might be. There is no wrong or right answer, so let your imagination run wild! (Our answer at the back of the book)

Animal Magic

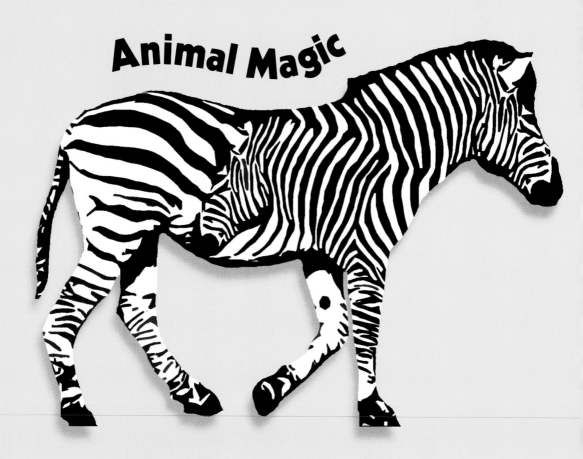

Can you see a second zebra hidden in the stripes of the main one?

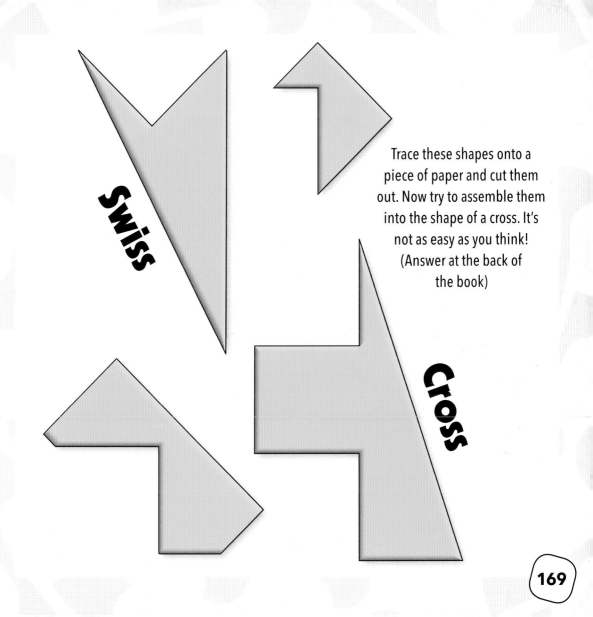

Swiss

Cross

Trace these shapes onto a piece of paper and cut them out. Now try to assemble them into the shape of a cross. It's not as easy as you think! (Answer at the back of the book)

Spiral Snail

The shell of this snail looks like one big spiral ... but is it?
Look again and you will see that it is actually made
up of lots of circles, each inside the other.

Hide and Seek

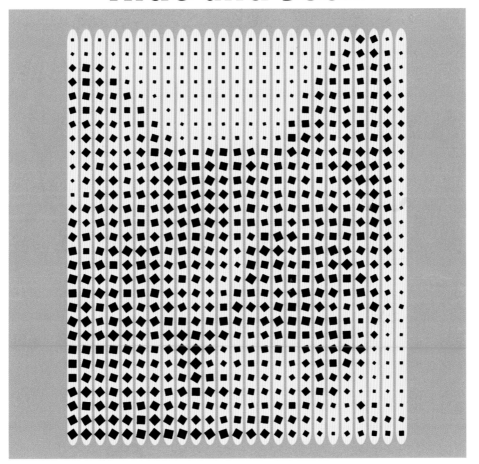

Prop the book up with this page open and walk away from it. As you get further away from it can you see something start to appear?

Which of these bowling balls is larger?
Remember, this is a book of optical
illusions, so think carefully!
(Answer at the back of the book)

Bowling Balls

The Cheshire Cat

Can you see a cat in the middle of the blue area? To make it disappear, close one eye and stare at the blue area for 15–20 seconds. If you keep staring the cat will reappear.

Lively Leprechaun

1 2 3 4 5 6

Hold this page about 30 cm in front of you and close your right eye. Focus on a number at a time, starting with 1, and count up slowly. By the time you reach 4, the leprechaun will have disappeared.

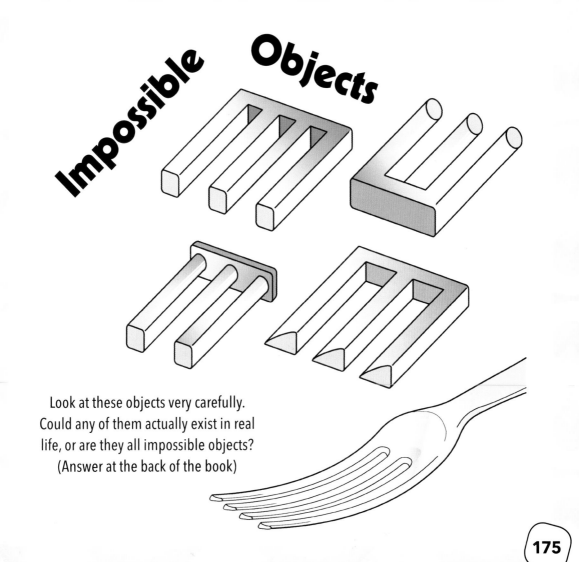

Impossible Objects

Look at these objects very carefully.
Could any of them actually exist in real
life, or are they all impossible objects?
(Answer at the back of the book)

Happy

At first glance these look like two normal dogs, but look again and you'll see they are a bit muddled up!

Dogs

Wild Child

Can you spot the face of a boy hidden in the tiger's fur?
(Answer at the back of the book)

Fairer Pharaoh

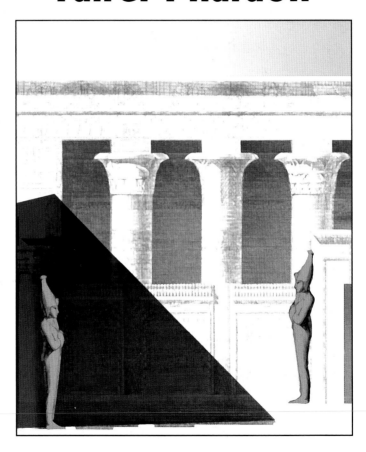

Can you crack this Egyptian boggler? Which of the statues
seems darker? (Answer at the back of the book)

Magic Wardrobe

Without measuring them, which green line looks longer: A–B or C–D? (Answer at the back of the book)

Tricky Triangles

How many triangles can you count here? Look very carefully, there are more than you think.
(Answer at the back of the book)

Bright Bulb

Is the yellow circle in the middle of this picture darker than its surround? What happens when you move it closer and further away from you? (Answer at the back of the book)

Waiting and Watching

Can you see a face watching this rower? Here's a clue: look under the bridge.

Leaning Tower Paintings

Crooked pictures can be very annoying. Can you make out which picture
of the Leaning Tower of Pisa in Italy is not hanging straight?
(Answer at the back of the book)

183

About Face

Is this woman facing sideways... or is she facing you, with her face half-hidden?

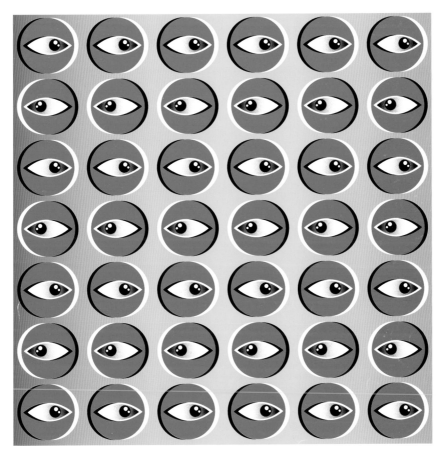

Shifty Eyes

Watch out! Whenever you look at one of these eyes,
you'll see the others shifting around.

High Roller

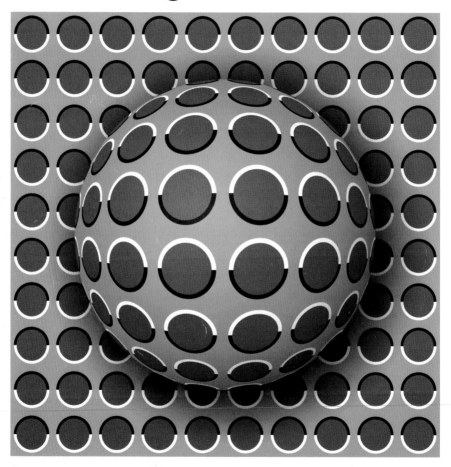

This ball never seems to stop rolling along, but it never gets anywhere.

Clowning Around

Does this clown's hair seem to magically grow outward?

Answers

p.34 It's a photo of a glass-windowed skyscraper reflecting the sky, set against a different photo of the sky.

p.44 It's a sundial.

p.67 The two cubes that form a bar across the middle can be removed to make this figure possible.

p.76 There are 59 'V's in the centre circle.

p.94 It's on the right edge of the hawk's left wing.

p.98 Arrows
There are eight arrows altogether, did you find them all?

p.99 Ant Army
You probably thought there were more white ants, but there are actually equal numbers of red and white ants.

p.100 Light or Heavy
The answer is neither! It's an optical illusion and the balance is perfectly level.

p.101 Crazy Wavy
If you check each line with a ruler you will find that they are all straight.

p.102 Famous Face
Did you find the famous painting of the Mona Lisa?

p.103 Spaghetti Twist
All the lines are straight and none of them bulge in any way.

p.104 Up the Garden Path
If you measure them with a ruler you will find they are the same length.

p.105 Van Cram
All the boxes will fit in the van.

p.106 Hidden in the Petals
It's a dolphin, did you find it?

p.107 All Alone?
Look carefully at the shape created by each cat's tail and back leg and you will see the faces of five people.

p.109 Towering Temples
Both temples A and B are the same height.

p.110 Shh, Someone's Listening!
Turn the book around and you will be able to see a face in the mountains behind the man.

p.113 Dog or Cat?
To find the cat turn the page upside down.

p.116 Golden Dome
Would you believe the answer is C and D!

p.117 Stripe Selection
The bar is actually the same colour all the way along, so the answer is A.

p.118 Bendy Legs
They are straight! It is the lines in the circles that make them appear bent.

p.119 Fourth Arrow
Did you get it right?

p.122 A Foxy Puzzle
The three hidden animals are shown by the circles. Did you find any human faces too? There are lots hidden in the picture!

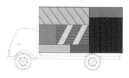

p.128 Hidden Baby
The baby panda is to the right of the mother, in the weeds.

p.129 Lonely Dancers
There is a large face in the centre of the picture.

p.130 Carpet Capers
Both carpets are the same length – check it with a ruler to see!

p.131 Where You Bean?

p.133 Hovering Helicopters
If you concentrate on the circles the red line seems longer, but if you look at the helicopters then the blue line seems longer. In fact, the blue line is the longest of the two.

p.134 Tall and Small
Oddly, the man closest to you is the tallest.

p.136 How Many Angels?
There are two different pairs of angels!

p.141 Chicks in the Nest
You can see either four birds sitting in four nests and one standing on a branch, or four chicks and a mother bird. In all, there are ten birds!

p.142 The Perfect Circle
Yes it is, but the stars around it make it look flattened.

p.144 A Very Odd Place
1. The columns can be rounded or square.
2. The boy's cart is an impossible shape.
3. The fountain is both in front and behind the column.
4. The stairs seem to only go down.
5. The jet of water passes through the stair rail.

p.150 Tiger Tiger
The black and white photograph becomes coloured.

p.155 All Tied Up
The answer is C. The squares are alternately light and dark.

p.157 Box Clever

p.158 The Magic Glass
Just turn the page upside down and the glass looks as if it is no longer on the tray.

p.165 What is it?
We think it might be an elephant standing on its front legs, but you might see something else.

p.167 Guess the Picture
We think this might be two cats drinking from a bowl of milk. What did you come up with?

p.169 Swiss Cross
Did you get it right?

p.171 Hide and Seek
There's a cat hiding in this puzzle.

p.172 Bowling Balls
Both the balls are the same size. Surprised?

p.175 Impossible Objects
None of these objects could exist in real life.

p.177 Wild Child
The hidden boy's face is shown by a circle.

p.178 Fairer Pharaoh
They are both the same shade, but the dark background makes the statue on the left seem lighter.

p.179 Magic Wardrobe
Although the A–B line seems longer, the two lines are actually the same length. Go on, measure them!

p.180 Tricky Triangles
There are 11 triangles in total. Three small white triangles, three small coloured triangles, three large coloured triangles and two hidden triangles, see below.

p.181 Bright Bulb
The yellow colour is the same all over the picture, but the middle circle seems to get brighter as you move it closer and further away from you.

p.183 Leaning Tower Paintings
The painting on the right is the crooked one.

Picture Credits

The publishers would like to thank the following sources for their kind permission to reproduce the pictures in this book.

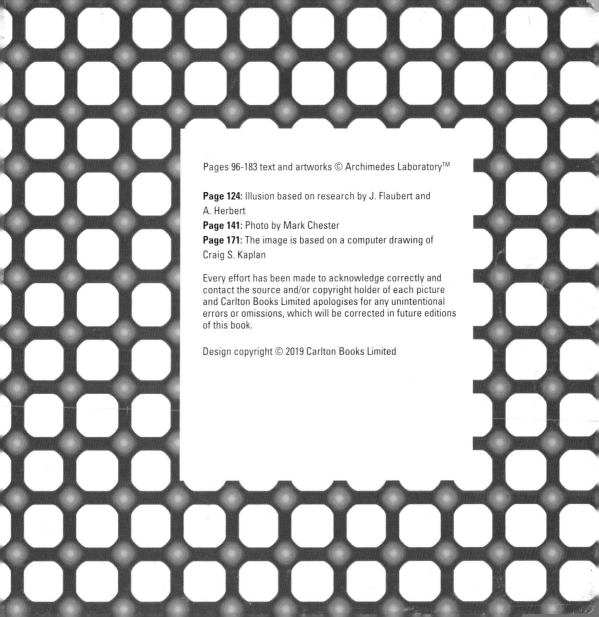

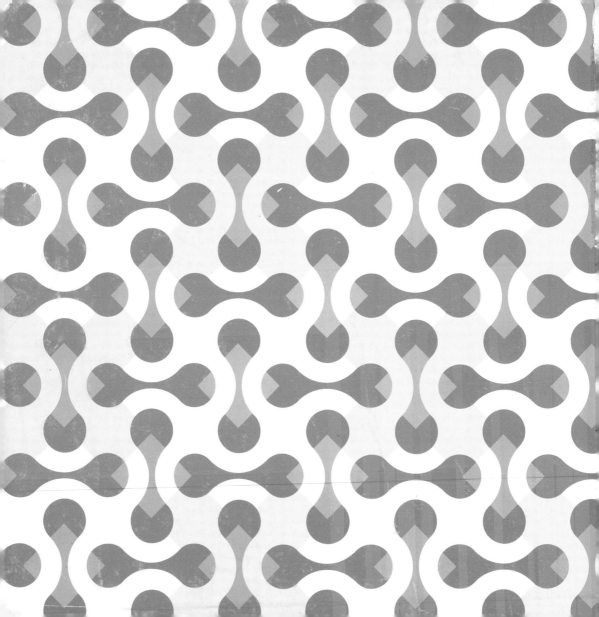